John West meets
Chief Peguis
October 1820

To the Glory of GOD and in
loving memory of Albert
and Ellen Le Beau

CHIEF PEGUIS
AND HIS DESCENDANTS

Chief Albert Edward Thompson,

A great great-grandson.

Peguis Publishers

462 Hargrave Street

Winnipeg, Man. R3A 0X5

1973

First published June 1973

ISBN 0-919566-20-0

Printed by Hignell Printing Limited.

CONTENTS

Chapter 1

This is the story of the famous Chief Peguis and a band of Saulteaux Indians who came from Sault Ste. Marie to the Red River country in the latter part of the 1790s.

The author is the great great-grandson of the Chief. This story was given to him in writing by his grandfather, the Reverend William Henry Prince. When the author left home in 1915 he laid it carefully away but, to his regret, it disappeared during his absence so that in telling this story he is relying on his memory.[1]

These people had no destination in mind when they left their old home in Ontario but decided to travel westward until they could find a location where fish, waterfowl and game could be had in abundance.

They travelled by canoe for weeks in their search, and finally entered Lake Winnipeg along the eastern shore and headed south, to the Red River. Not far from its mouth, the Saulteaux canoes came to a halt when they encountered a small stream flowing from the west.

On the banks of this stream a fairly large encampment was discovered which appeared to be deserted. After assuring themselves that this was not an ambush, a landing-party went forward to investigate. The teepees contained the remains of dead bodies.

It was evident that the people had succumbed to disease. Their tools, cooking pots, clothing and totems revealed a tribe unknown to Chief Peguis and his followers.

The Saulteaux paddled further along this "river of the dead" and came upon a second silent camp where the teepees also held corpses. When an alert scout observed a movement in the willows he found a small boy hiding. The frightened child told Peguis how his people, the Plains Cree, had sickened and died of smallpox. He was the lone survivor.[2]

The boy was adopted into the tribe and named Pockwa-now. They called the river Ne-poo-win, Death River. The white men named it Netley Creek.

The location seemed to be ideal for the band's needs. From the mouth of the Red to the creek fishing was good, and in the marshes on both sides of the river plenty of fur-bearing animals and wild fowl could be seen. There was also wild rice, and scrub maple trees that the people could tap for sugar in the spring, and fertile ground in which to plant the Indian corn that old Shag-koosink had carried in a deerskin bag from Sault Ste. Marie.

Now that the earlier occupants no longer required the area, the Saulteaux appropriated the land for their new home. Later when their explorations took them south along the Red to the mouth of the Assiniboine River, they found a large band of Indians encamped for the winter.

These were the Assiniboines, led by Chief Ouckidoat. They occupied the country stretching westward from the Red River far across the prairie. They subsisted wholly on the buffalo, and told the newcomers that they were welcome to the animals of the bushland and the fish in the waters.

Chief Peguis and Chief Ouckidoat smoked the pipe of peace and swore allegiance. Together, they would fight the Sioux, their common enemy since 1640, and jointly patrol the Red River, the route frequently used by their foe from the south. The Sioux, who claimed all the land about the Pembina River where it joins the Red (just south of the International Boundary) often made forays to plunder and kill as far north as the junction of the Red and the Assiniboine, known to voyageurs, fur traders and the Métis as the "Forks."

Returning to Netley Creek, the Saulteaux made preparations for their winter camp. From the inner bark of trees they braided a large net, some seventy feet long, weighted with stones. Several canoes carried it out into the water, where it was dropped, then slowly dragged back to shore filled with fish. The women prepared these for winter use by baking them in a long, low stone oven. They were then placed in birchbark or woven reed baskets, and buried in the ground to freeze. Bear-fat mixed with wild berries was also placed in the ground.

The women collected the largest shells from the lakeshore, filled them with fish and animal oil and a strip of rag to serve as lamps.

One hundred rabbits were killed for each family. The meat filled the cooking pots, and the skins were cut into strips and woven into mittens, blankets and hoods. The floors of the teepees were covered with animal skins and braided rushes, dyed with colour extracted from rocks and roots.

Medicinal plants such as wild ginger roots growing in abundance at the river's edge were dug and hung to dry. They would be used later in the treatment of colds and coughs. Seneca root was gathered by the midwives and a brew of the powdered herb administered to both human and canine mothers-to-be at the appropriate moment.

When roving bands arrived from the Great Lakes to visit and hunt on the Plains, they were made welcome by the Saulteaux encampment. With one of these groups there appeared a large bark canoe bearing a flag denoting the royal status of the occupant, Princess Net-no-kwa.[3]

Recently widowed, she was travelling with her two sons. Her husband had lived in the Red River country when a young boy and often spoke of the fabulous prairie black with herds of buffalo, and the princess was hopeful of her sons becoming rich in the hunt.

Chief Peguis, observing the white skin of a fourteen-year-old boy, learned that he had been kidnapped from the settlers in Ohio six years before. He answered to the

Indian name Shaw-Shaw-was-Be-na-se or The Falcon and appeared quite devoted to his foster-mother and older brother. His real name was John Tanner.

When Peguis saw Tanner eight years later, in 1803, the "white Indian" was twenty-two years old. He was one of a party of braves gathered at Fort Pembina to avenge a massacre there. A minor Assiniboine chief, the father-in-law of Alexander Henry the Younger, who was in charge of the Nor'Wester's fort, had been shot as he sat in a tree scanning the prairie for signs of buffalo.

Before the party of raiding Sioux could be driven off a number of men, women and children had been slaughtered.

When Alexander Henry returned from an inspection trip and found the people in mourning, he supplied the avenging Assiniboine and the Saulteaux with guns and ammunition, to pursue and fight the Sioux.

Peguis and his warriors joined the battle to annihilate the invaders, and the Chief noticed that John Tanner fought beside his adopted brother with outstanding bravery.[4]

Enroute to Fort Pembina to aid the Assiniboines, the Saulteaux left the old men, women and children in a grove of trees known as Seven Oaks, not far from the Forks, to await the return of the warriors.

After the battle at Fort Pembina when the Sioux were badly beaten, Chief Peguis and his braves rejoined their wives and children and rested there for a time before returning to Netley Creek.

Three warriors were missing, and presumed dead.

Their companions had searched the area without success. Among the missing was one called Misko-me-oopan. This man was seriously wounded and fell by the wayside, unnoticed by the others. Regaining consciousness after some time, he carefully examined his wounds, then decided to search for water, which he badly needed. As he crawled towards the river bank he noticed someone lying on the ground nearby.

He recognized the man as one of his comrades, and this knowledge renewed his strength and he struggled towards his friend. As he drew near, Misko-me-oo-pan found to his amazement that his friend had tried to hang himself by fastening a belt around his neck and securing the other end to a small poplar. Fortunately the tree was not strong enough, and he was too weak to reach another larger poplar.

Misko-me-oo-pan reached him and gave what help he could. Suddenly the two men heard a noise close at hand. They discovered a third warrior belonging to their tribe, crawling towards them through the bush.

The three men now discussed plans to reach home, and decided that they must in some way make a raft on which they could float downstream on the Red River. This they managed to construct from dry driftwood lying around, and, as the water was high, the current of the river was strong enough to carry them along. They had no food, and their only weapon was one flintlock gun with some powder and one bullet for ammunition.

Luck was in their favour. As they floated down the river they came across a young buffalo on the shore which had just been killed by a bear. By firing at the bear they managed to frighten him away, and were able to get small portions of the buffalo meat to the raft.

A few stops were made along the way for rest periods. At one place they came across a teepee by the riverbank. Crawling cautiously to it, they discovered that it was deserted but contained enough sleeping robes and ammunition to serve them for the remainder of the journey home. Finally, late one day they came within sight of the Indian encampment at Seven Oaks. Here they camped for the night, as they did not dare go further until daylight for fear they might be mistaken for enemies and shot by their own tribesmen before they could be recognized.

The next day a shirt was raised for a flag, to let their comrades know that they were friends. They were met by Peguis and accepted as true warriors and heroes. A pow-wow was held which lasted two days and nights to honour their bravery and the good work they had done.

Later the Chief and his people returned to their original settlement at Netley Creek, and lived there, not too peacefully at first, but after a few years all went well.

Chief Peguis was now thirty years old, and a very impressive figure when, on special occasions, he donned a feathered war-bonnet and fringed and beaded tunic. For ordinary wear he was attired simply in breech cloth and red leggings with a blanket over one shoulder. His long braids were studded with bits of brass, and despite the fact that he had lost part of his nose in a fight his appearance was striking.

My great great-grandfather often told his children and grandchildren how his disfiguration came about, and the whole incident is well described by John Tanner who was an eye-witness to the event.

Tanner's brother, Wa-me-gon-abiew, along with several other young hunters, drank too freely while trading at Fort Pembina, and when they saw the son of Chief Tabush-shik beating an old woman, Wa-me-gon-abiew caught hold of the bully's arms to restrain him. Tanner wrote in his book:

> At that moment Chief Tabush-shik misapprehending the nature of my brother's interference seized him by the hair and bit off his nose. Chief Peguis entered the scuffle and Wa-me-gon-abiew perceiving the loss of his own nose, suddenly raised his hands and seizing the head that was nearest to him bit off the nose! But Be-wag-is (Tanner's spelling of Peguis) is a kind and good man and being aware of the erroneous impression under which my brother had acted never for a moment betrayed anything like anger or resentment. "I am an old man (he was thirty-six) and it is but a short time that they will laugh at me for the loss of my nose."[5]

Chapter 2

In the early 1800s the fur trade was in full swing. The Hudson's Bay Company and the North West Company were rivals, each dealing with the Indians in their own territory. My ancestors dealt with the Hudson's Bay Company, and continued to do so through the years.

Trouble soon started when the Hudson's Bay Company sold Lord Selkirk 116,000 acres of land about the Forks on which to place his settlers from Scotland.

The North West Company feared that this would destroy the fur trade and were determined to run the Selkirk Settlers out of the country.

Our people watched the first white settlers arrive by H B C York boats in the summer of 1812. These were all men sent ahead to plow some land and build log cabins for the families expected the following year.

Due to misunderstandings and disasters, they did not arrive until the autumn of 1814 — a party of sixty-three men, women and children. There were cabins built but no crops or gardens planted.[1] The Hudson's Bay Company store within Fort Douglas could not supply the newcomers with winter provisions. This meant that the Selkirk Settlers had to follow the example of the Indians and join the buffalo hunt some sixty miles south to Pembina.

The Saulteaux rode their ponies alongside the weary line of settlers walking over the snowy prairie and frozen streams. Our people took pity on the exhausted parents carrying small children, and offered to carry them to Pembina.

The Scottish people must have been very frightened of losing their children as the warriors and hunters, usually gaily feathered and painted to whatever mood they were enjoying, galloped away out of sight. Days later when the distraught parents reached the little village of forts about the Pembina River, they found without exception, all the children had been safely delivered. Many of the fathers and mothers repaid the Indians with gifts of jewelry and warm shawls.

This created a strong bond of faith and respect between the Saulteaux and the Selkirk Settlers that was never broken by either side. The white settlers accompanied these hunters on their winter treks for six or seven years because of lack of food to carry them and their families through the winter months.

On June 22, 1815 Cuthbert Grant and William Shaw put the first torches to the settlers' cabins. Chief Peguis, alarmed at this action, tried to intervene but without success. My ancestors often told the story of how sad it made their parents to see the defenceless white people scurry down to their dugout boats and start on the long journey to Norway House. They intended to spend the winter there and reach Hudson Bay the following summer in time to catch a sailing vessel back to Scotland.

On their arrival at Norway House they found another party of Scottish Settlers on their way to the Red River Colony (now in ashes). This group was led by Colin Robertson, a former Nor'Wester who was now in the employ of the Hudson's Bay Company. Robertson had eighty-four new settlers and forty labourers, who, with the refugee Scots from the destroyed Colony made a formidable company. He led them back to Red River, arriving on August 19th, again too late to replant the crops and gardens destroyed by the Nor'Westers.

Colin Robertson met with the Métis at the Forks and convinced them that the Colony was not a threat to the fur trade, rather an additional market, and the winter months passed without trouble.

But the Nor'Westers under Cuthbert Grant were more resolved than ever to destroy the Colony "beyond renewal".

Twenty-one Hudson's Bay Company men and a few settlers were massacred by the Nor'Westers at Seven Oaks on June 18, 1816.

Chief Peguis, who was camped with his warriors across the Red, watched the battle, and held those in check who might have joined the fight. After the killings, the Nor'Westers burned the homes of the settlers and their crops and galloped on ponies after the fleeing people, shouting to them to leave Red River and never return.[2]

At dusk Chief Peguis entered Fort Douglas and approached Madame Marie-Anne Lajimonière, wife of the buffalo-hunter, who had taken refuge with her children in the fort.

"Frenchwoman, hear me. The Métis will take this fort in the morning. Leave this place tonight and I will save you and your children. Come to my tent on the other side of the river where you will be safe."[3]

When it was dark Madame Lajimonière hurried her family out of the fort and down to the river where Peguis and two women waited in a canoe. Marie-Anne had been so alarmed by the day's senseless killings, that she fainted as she stepped into the light craft, and all were thrown into the water. Many hands reached out in the darkness, and the little French-Canadian family was saved.

Madame Lajimonière's husband, Jean Baptiste, after Cuthbert Grant's mandate to the settlers the year before, set out for Montreal to inform Lord Selkirk of the threat to his Colony and the dire circumstances in which the Scottish farmers found themselves. Now she was entirely dependent upon Chief Peguis.

The morning after her escape from Fort Douglas, it was occupied by the Métis, and the Hudson's Bay Company employees were banished also. While the Métis were engaged in this heartless act, Peguis and his men gathered the mutilated bodies that had been left to the wolves at Seven Oaks, and buried them in a little grove of trees close to the fort. Governor Semple and the company doctor were laid in rough boxes; the others were wrapped in Indian blankets. Eye-witnesses reported that Chief

Peguis stood at the burial with tears running down his cheeks. These white men were his friends. They had been outnumbered three to one, and no mercy had been shown the wounded.

The Chief reached Netley Creek almost as quickly as the homeless settlers, and at the Saulteaux village they were fed corn and meat. By now, thoroughly chastened, the Scottish farmers planned to sail down Lake Winnipeg and take refuge at Norway House once more for the winter, then take the summer boats for Hudson Bay.

Chief Peguis supplied them with fish and wild rice. They were completely at the mercy of the Saulteaux, having only what they were wearing at the time of the attack.

Madame Lajimonière spent the summer with Peguis' family — four wives and seven children. When winter came and the Métis hunters returned to their homes at Pembina, she moved into her log hut on the banks of the Assiniboine River. The Saulteaux hunters kept her supplied with meat.

Jean Baptiste returned from Montreal a few days before Christmas. He had a very adventurous story to tell of his trip.

Selkirk immediately engaged a force of Swiss soldiers known as the de Meurons, under the leadership of Captain D'Orsonnens, and the small army marched westward. Lajimonière and his Indian companion made faster progress than the soldiers, and the buffalo-hunter predicted that they would arrive within a week to recapture Fort

Douglas. Lord Selkirk would travel by canoe when the rivers opened.

Captain D'Orsonnens, aware that the Indians about Rainy River used a trail to the Northwest known to them as the "old muskeg carrying place" persuaded John Tanner, who was wintering in the area, to guide the soldiers overland to the Red River.[4]

In early January 1817 Chief Peguis' scouts reported the approach of the de Meurons. With a number of his best warriors the Chief rode out to join the troops about ten miles south of the Forks. It was after midnight when the soldiers approached Fort Douglas and found no outdoor guards.

Chief Peguis held his men in readiness for action within the pallisades should it be necessary. They stood by and gleefully watched the Swiss soldiers, under Tanner's guidance, place Indian ladders against the walls of the fort. (These were sturdy trees from which the branches had been lopped off at either side to make footholds or steps.)

The de Meurons made a bloodless conquest and reclaimed the territory for the Hudson's Bay Company. Peguis' warriors had enjoyed a good show although they had anticipated inflicting smarting punishment on the Nor'Westers to avenge Seven Oaks.

Chief Peguis, whenever he detected signs of restlessness among the young braves, would dash his knife into the ground and cry angrily, "So will I deal with them who disobey my orders!"

Chapter 3

At nine o'clock on the morning of June 21, 1817 Lord Selkirk and a fleet of thirty canoes reached Netley Creek. He had a bodyguard of seven soldiers wearing bright red coats that impressed the Saulteaux very much. There were thirty-seven soldiers of the de Meuron and de Wattville regiments. It was an impressive display of colour and force that pleased Chief Peguis and his band.

The Chief with his warriors accompanied Lord Selkirk along the Red River to Fort Douglas. He offered to drive all the Métis serving under Cuthbert Grant away but Lord Selkirk refused to use force.[1]

He sent his agent to Norway House to lure the destitute settlers back to the Colony. While he awaited their return, Lord Selkirk laid out excellent plans for an entire township. There would be roads, churches, schools and two-mile long farm lots stretching back from the rivers. Teachers and clergymen of all denominations were also promised for the new settlement.

Lord Selkirk met with Chief Peguis and four other men of influence among their people to discuss the situation. One lesson had been learned from the tragic Seven Oaks massacre — the original inhabitants of the

Plains must be consulted and reimbursed for loss of their hunting-grounds to the colonists.

When agreement was reached, Lord Selkirk placed the name of Chief Peguis above that of Ouckidoat, Rayagie, Reboma, Muchiwikoab and Mukitoukoonace, although the Crees and the Assiniboines had occupied this part of the country long before the arrival of the Saulteaux.

In exchange for the 116,000 acres of land acquired by Lord Selkirk for his settlers, the tribes were to receive presents or quit-rents annually as follows —

> To the Chiefs and Warriors of the Chippewas or Saulteaux nation, one-hundred pounds of good marketable tobacco to be delivered on, or before the 10th day of October at Fort Douglas. To the Chiefs and Warriors of the Kinistino or Cree nations, a like present or quit-claim of one-hundred pounds of tobacco to be delivered on or before the 19th day of October at Portage la Prairie on the banks of the Assiniboine River.
>
> July 18th, in the 57th year of the reign of King George III, and in the year of our Lord 1817.[2]

Lord Selkirk was very grateful for the loyal and generous way Chief Peguis treated the first settlers. He knew that if the Chief had joined forces with the Nor'-Westers the white families could have been killed or starved or driven far away, perhaps never to return to Red River. He was so pleased with my great great-grandfather's concern for the Selkirk Settlers that he presented him with a large silver medal. It bore the likeness of King George III on one side and the Hudson's Bay Company crest on the other. The more practical gift of a warm red coat trimmed with gold braid pleased Peguis even more. The fine coat has long since disappeared but the silver medal may be seen in the Manitoba Museum of Man and Nature.

During the weeks that Lord Selkirk waited for the return of the settlers he and Peguis saw a good deal of one another, and the Scottish lord realized how much his colonists owed to his willingness to give them food and to make certain that the white people were not harassed by the half-breeds and unfriendly Indians.

He gave Peguis a letter of introduction that would assure him of hospitality wherever he travelled:

The Bearer, Peguis, one of the principal chiefs of the Chippewas or Saulteaux of Red River, has been a steady friend to the Settlement ever since its first establishment and has never deserted its cause in its greatest reverses. He has often exerted his influence to restore peace; and having rendered most essential services to the settlers in their distress, deserves to be treated with favour and distinction by the officers of the Hudson's Bay Company and all friends of peace and order. Selkirk. Fort Douglas, July 17, 1817.[3]

A few days before Lord Selkirk's departure from Red River Peguis visited the fort and reported to the Scottish earl, "The half-breeds have plotted to kill you. They asked me to bring a bag of pemmican to their place of ambush but I refused and told them that I would prevent this killing."

. Chief Peguis said, "Lord Selkirk was very happy that I had saved his life."[4]

When the settlers returned from Norway House Chief Peguis greeted them warmly, and through the lean years provided buffalo meat for the little Colony. Naturally he became their good friend and every home was open to him. He quickly learned the dates of their festivals, weddings and baptisms, and with a few favourites of his band, would journey to the settlement to join in the merriment and feasting.

Whenever he imbibed too freely Peguis liked to tell the Scots that he was going to the fort to frighten the Governor, particularly if the man in power was not popular. All enjoyed the joke and the fact that Peguis called himself the Colony Chief.

He was terribly angered, however, when one of his warriors carried the trick a step further. When intoxicated he thrust himself into the Governor's quarters and ripped off his coat. The Indian then drew his knife and threatened to kill the Governor.

The Chief's great sense of fairness allowed him to agree that the white man carry out his own type of punishment on the foolish warrior.

Chapter 4

It was in late September 1820, while the Reverend John West, the first Protestant minister to reach Red River, was having breakfast with the Hudson's Bay Company boatmen at Netley Creek, that Chief Peguis approached the little group of travellers. He greeted the missionary from England with characteristic courtesy, "I wish that more of the stumps and brushwood were cleared away from your feet on coming to see my country."[1]

When he drew Lord Selkirk's parchment from his beaded vest John West said gravely, "I am sorry to tell you that your friend, His Lordship, died in France last April."

Peguis was quite saddened by this information and touched the big silver medal he wore around his neck as fondly as he would have taken the hand of his friend, the Silver Chief.

Some time later when passing through the Netley encampment John West wrote in his journal, "Peguis came with his eldest son and another Indian to drink tea with me in the evening." While they smoked, the clergyman impressed upon the Chief the benefits available to Indian children sent to the mission school at Fort Douglas.

"What will you do with the children after they have been taught what you wish them to know?"

John West replied that it was the white man's hope that they would turn to agriculture and the Christian way of life. "A man should have only one woman, and a woman one husband."

Peguis smiled. "I think there is no more harm in Indians having two wives than one of the settlers at Red River." Which he named.[2]

When amalgamation of the Hudson's Bay Company and the North West Company took place in 1821, Nicholas Garry as Governor of the older company, and Simon McGillivray representing the North West Trading Company, made a trip from Montreal to Red River to settle details of the merger.

Garry recorded their arrival, in separate canoes, in his diary:

Friday, August 3, 1821. We arrived at the Encampment of the Indians who have cultivated fields of Corn Indian. Their chief is called Cut Nose from having lost a part of his nose in an affray. He is a good-looking man of fifty, has always been a great friend of the Colony and once actually defended it from the attacks of their blood-thirsty enemies. The chief's daughter is very pretty. The Cut Nose is anxious that Mr. Bird's son should marry her. The young men were gone on a war-party to attack their enemies the Sioux.[3]

Three days later Nicholas Garry wrote,

Aug. 6, Monday. At half-past nine arrived at the Encampment of Pegqas or Cut Nose. The Chief had his flag hoisted, an English Jack with the H B C arms, given to him by Lord Selkirk. He showed me testimony written on Moosehide stating that he had always been a faithful, sincere friend to the Colony . . . . Mr. McGillivray told Chief Peguis he was a bad Indian for having defended the Colony.

The Reverend John West incurred the disapproval of Governor Simpson when he criticized his amorous affairs with native women and the use of liquor in the fur trade.

John West returned to England in 1823. Though many others came to the Settlement after him, three Anglican missionaries were especially respected by the Saulteaux — David Jones in 1824, William Cockran in 1825, and John Smithurst in 1839.

All three men were sent by the Anglican Church Missionary Society to work among the settlers at Red River and to carry the word of God to the Indians whenever possible.

In 1829 my great great-grandfather met the man who was to become his closest white friend and who exerted a good influence on all my ancestors, the Reverend William Cockran.

The missionary was working on the land at Image Plains just west of the farms belonging to the Kildonan settlers, and had engaged several young Indian boys with bows

21

and arrows to keep the blackbirds and wild pigeons away from the corn.

When I was working on the land I was visited by Chief Peguis. I explained why the land was cultivated. He looked at me with a satirical smile and pointed to the river and the plains to show me where his wealth lay.

Cockran gave the Chief some pemmican and ammunition, and "he left promising that he would return and eat some beef with me in the winter."[4]

Cockran's duties required him to preach at the Upper Church at Fort Garry by the Forks, and at the Lower Church at St. Andrew's Rapids (Now Lockport). He was a man wholly without subterfuge and never stood aloof on the sidelines or permitted an injustice because the offender might not lie within his jurisdiction.

In 1829 Cockran moved his home from the Red River Settlement down to the St. Andrew's Rapids. He was convinced that there was greater need for both spiritual and material teaching around the southern end of Lake Winnipeg. Although he had to retain his office of chaplain to the men of the Hudson's Bay Company at Fort Garry, by the Forks (this now replaced Fort Douglas) the missionary travelled twenty miles on horseback back and forth between the two places.

I should say that while the Reverend William Cockran is best remembered perhaps for the five churches that he built between Portage la Prairie and St. Peter's north of the town of Selkirk, my people remember him best for the way in which he dedicated his life to the betterment of their daily lives.

His aim was to enable the Saulteaux to become independent of the hunt that would be good one season and very poor the next. He showed us the advantages of building permanent log cabins and planting sufficient vegetables and grain to stave off starvation when wild game was scarce. As settlement increased over the years good hunting decreased.

In 1832 he approached Governor Simpson for approval of his plan to teach the Saulteaux farming. When the Governor agreed, Cockran made week-long visits to our Netley encampment and got Chief Peguis' permission to instruct the people how to till the land, even offering to supply gardening implements, seed potato, barley and other grains.

Through Joseph Cook, Cockran's interpreter, he made a stirring speech:

Six times has this river frozen since I came to your country and as many times it has opened again. Six times have the flocks of wild fowl passed and repassed. I diminish not their number nor retard their flight. Yet you see I have enough. Every time you have passed my house I have fed you when hungry. I have enough to feed my family, my servants, the Indian children and the passing strangers. Now, if you let me farm at your village it shall be entirely for the benefit of yourself and tribe. I will teach you. I will supply you with hoes and seed. I will send a man with oxen to plow the land. I will help you to build comfortable homes.

That winter, 1832-33, our band felt the pinch of poverty as never before. Peguis was heavily in debt, overdrawn at the trading-post to the amount of three-hundred muskrat skins. Now nearly sixty years of age, Peguis lacked the agility and stamina required of the hunter. His wives and their children had to be clothed and fed, and he was not able to follow the buffalo miles to the west or south.

More than once that bitter winter he appeared at the missionary's door begging for food, "Not for myself but for my children."

By spring the Chief had won his counsellors over and he permitted William Cockran to move into the Saulteaux village to teach the people how to make a living off the land.

Cockran built his own home, and a cabin that served as both school and church, at Sugar Point directly across the Red River from Netley Creek. Here Mrs. Cockran taught the young girls to spin flax and keep a tidy house. John Garrioch taught the Indian boys simple carpentry and to read and write.

The missionary often conducted classes of his own, showing the Indian boys how to gather hay with which to stuff mattresses and how to handle farm implements.

A great feast was arranged at Netley in the autumn of 1832 to celebrate their first harvest, to which Cockran was invited. It was held in October in the largest teepee, the conjuror's. William Cockran described the scene:

The whole of the tent was hung with pieces of ribbon and cloth; the men and women who were admitted to the dance each hung up the best that he had — all these were presents to the conjuror. The Chief's daughter who is always civil was much more so today. She would not let me leave the tent until she had cooked some bear-meat that I might partake of the feast.

That fall, Cockran hired three dependable men to help him build a log cabin for the Chief on Sugar Point. My forefathers called it by this name because of the maple trees there that the people tapped each spring for syrup.

The Chief's hut "was completed October 3rd, except for the mudding" between the logs, and Peguis soon moved into it. Another Saulteaux named Red Deer came to Cockran with fifty bushels of potatoes as payment for a similar home. But the missionary told him he must engage men himself to do the work.

The following year William Cockran recorded "the commencement of a fine new fort at St. Andrew's Rapids." This was the Stone Fort or Lower Fort Garry, as it came to be known.[5]

When his wife died, David Jones returned to England with his small children. Enroute to Hudson Bay he stopped to bid farewell to Peguis. The Chief handed Jones a letter to be "delivered to the missionary men in England."

This was a mild rebuke from the Saulteaux to the Church Missionary Society. Now that they had accepted the Christian way of life and sent their children to the missionaries' school, the Society was taking away their preacher-teachers. David Jones would not be returning to Red River and William Cockran was planning to open a mission school at Portage la Prairie where none yet existed.

The letter from the Saulteaux read in part:

Surely 300 souls is worthy of one Praying Master. Can it be expected that once or twice teaching of a child can be sufficient to make him wise or to enable him to guide himself through life? No, our friends and we are the same. We all wish to let you know, as Mr. Cockran began with us we wish him to end with us. He is well-accustomed with our oily and fishy smell and all our bad habits.

Chief Red Eagle, son and successor of Chief Peguis. Signed Treaty No. 1 at Lower Fort Garry in 1871. *Courtesy Provincial Archives of Manitoba.*

John, "Long Jake", third son of Red Eagle, and Life Councillor at St. Peter's Reserve. In 1885 as his father's proxy, signed agreement with Canadian Government in Ottawa, regarding St. Peter's Reserve land dispute. *Courtesy Provincial Archives of Manitoba.*

Chapter 5

It was Peguis' custom each New Year's Day to visit the Red River Settlement to receive hospitality at the homes of the settlers. Further along the trail leading to the Forks, the Chief and his headmen paid their respects to Governor Simpson in residence at Upper Fort Garry.

On January 1, 1835 Governor Simpson presented the Chief with a testimonial written on a square of buffalo-hide that would endure for years. With this parchment was a gift of five pound-sterling, the equivalent of $50 at that time.

These are to certify that Pegowis, the Saulteaux Chief has uniformly been friendly to the Whites, well disposed towards the Settlement of Red River and altogether a steady and intelligent and well-conducted Indian. In consideration of these facts and being now in the decline of life unable to maintain himself and family by the produce of the chase alone, it is hereby certified that I have assured him of an annuity for life from the Honourable Hudson's Bay Company of five pound sterling commencing with a payment of that amount this day. Fort Garry,

27

1st of January 1835. Geo. Simpson, Governor of Rupert's Land.[1]

It was in the summer of 1838 that my great great-grandfather was converted. The Reverend William Cockran had listened to his desire to become a Christian for almost four years but the missionary said that the Chief must first give up all intoxicating liquor, and most difficult of all, reduce his wives to one legal mate.

After four years of total abstinence — and Cockran fully realized the strong temptation Peguis faced whenever he visited the friendly settlers — Chief Peguis was admitted into the Anglican Church. Many of his followers also accepted the new God.

In honour of the occasion William Cockran gave the Chief a large Bible. It was greatly prized and handed down from one generation to another. So much was it handled that today it bears only one name — "Sarah Bella Parisiene. Born Sept. 12, 1902."[2]

The Parisiene family married into the Peguis clan soon after the Chief's old friend, Baptiste Parisiene, made a fine chair for Peguis, now aging and quite deaf. It was whittled with a pen-knife from a strong piece of oak driftwood.[3]

On Christmas Day 1839 William Cockran welcomed the Reverend John Smithurst from England, assigned to serve at the Indian Settlement at Sugar Point, now named St. Peter's by the missionary. Cockran had hoped that the new clergyman would be his assistant in this large field but since he was still officially chaplain for the Hudson's Bay Company, William Cockran was requested to return to St. Andrew's Rapids to live where so many retired officers of the Company had built stone houses near the Lower Fort. My ancestors were deeply saddened by this move but they often visited Cockran at the Rapids where he was building a fine stone church and home. John Smithurst wrote in his journal —

Jan. 11, 1840. I was sitting at breakfast when I learned that Chief Peguis' eldest son had committed suicide. . . . From the time his father and three younger brothers embraced Christianity he had tried to deprive his father of the Chieftainship.

A well-known Manitoba author, Nan Shipley, writing in the Manitoba Pageant, September 1956, in an article writes:

PEGUIS FRIEND OF THE PALE FACE Without the friendship of this remarkable Indian, the settlement at the Forks of the Red and the Assiniboine Rivers could not have been established as early as 1812. . . . . In spite of the fact that he had part of his nose bitten off in a fight, Peguis was quite handsome, and possessed gifts of great oratory and physical prowess.

Peguis watched the beginnings of the Selkirk Settlement and noticed the resentment of the Nor'-westers who considered the Colony as encroachment on their territory. He saw, too, the rivalry between the two great fur trade companies, and warned his people against taking sides.

On June 19, 1816, Governor Semple and 21

men were ambushed and killed at Seven Oaks, midway between Kildonan and the Settlement. Farm houses were burned, crops were destroyed and settlers routed. They received temporary protection from Peguis as they fled north, but continued on to Norway House where they spent the winter. Afterwards an officer of the Nor'westers chided Peguis for not helping to drive out the settlers. "You Indians should have joined forces with us to drive them off your land." Peguis proved his generosity and concern for the plight of the settlers by making gifts of fish and wild rice, when they returned to their ruined farms the following spring, and for many years afterwards he supplied them with buffalo meat.

The year following the Seven Oaks massacre, Lord Selkirk visited the Red River and made a treaty with the Indians of the district. Peguis and four others signed the treaty by their marks — a rough drawing of an animal that signified their private totem or coat-of-arms. Chief Peguis' signature resembled a large wolf. . . .

A year from the signing of the treaty with Lord Selkirk, Peguis led 34 canoes to the Fort to receive the promised gift of tobacco. He also signed his mark to deeds of land some of the settlers purchased from him at this time.

In describing the suicide of Chief Peguis' eldest son Nan Shipley goes on to say —

When the young warrior quarrelled with his father, he and a dozen followers moved twenty miles from Sugar Point. The young man's daughter died, and in grief he hung himself from a tree behind his teepee.

The dead man's friends prepared his body for burial and returned it to his father, as this was the custom in those days.

Chief Peguis, crushed by the Christian regulations that would not permit a heathen suicide to be buried in hallowed ground, was deeply saddened. He stripped his son's body of its traditional trappings — red feathers from the long black hair, red paint from the cold face, beads of the same colour from ears and nostrils — and placed the body in a coffin as close as possible to the fence of the St. Peter's churchyard.

On October 7, 1840 the Reverend John Smithurst legally married Chief Peguis and his wife of many years. She took the name Victoria after the Queen of England. The Chief was registered as William King: the surname in recognition of his position in the tribe, and William in admiration of William Cockran.

"My sons are now princes, and shall be known by that name."[4]

None of his descendants used the name King. We were all known by the name Prince.

Then, in 1841, Peguis learned that James Evans, a Methodist missionary stationed at Norway House, had invented the Cree Syllabics, a simple form of shorthand that made it possible for the Indians to read and write their own language for the first time. Always alert for the fresh and new approach to any important changes as they affected his people, he took a dozen of his most intelligent young men the entire length of Lake Winnipeg to investigate this marvel.

Peguis met the inventor at Norway House, and James Evans taught the Chief and his men the thirty-six marks or symbols by which the alphabet of any dialect could be quickly memorized and adapted to any native tongue.

Peguis was in his late eighties, in June of 1859, when the banks of the Red River at the Settlement echoed with the cheers of the people as they watched the arrival of the first steamboat, the *S.S. Anson Northup*.

Four years later, on October 14, 1863 *The Nor'Wester* newspaper carried a two-column editorial entitled — "Important Statement of Pegowis."

In this the Chief maintained that the treaty he and four others signed with Lord Selkirk in the summer of 1817, did not constitute surrender of their lands.

"Lord Selkirk promised to come back and negotiate about our land. But Lord Selkirk never came back." He had died in 1820. "He never came back to complete the arrangements for our land. Our lands have not been bought, we have not received payment for them."

The tobacco distributed annually to the Saulteaux at the Red River Settlement, and to the Crees at Portage la Prairie — "was only a goodwill token... I told Lord Selkirk, 'I will give you the bend of the river (Red) above Sugar Point. That point I like very much. I cannot part with it. It is for my children.' This satisfied Lord Selkirk."[5]

Chief Peguis died, at about age ninety, in the mellow Indian summer September 28, 1864. He was given a funeral usually accorded only the highest dignitaries of the land. Two archdeacons officiated and people from all religious denominations and walks of life attended. Chief Peguis had been in this part of the country longer than any white man present.

In October 1924 a fine stone was erected over the grave of Chief Peguis in St. Peter's churchyard. The Rev. William Henry Prince was chosen to represent the famous chief, his grandfather. This was the largest gathering held at St. Peter's church.

On his tombstone is carved the following tribute:

In memory of Peguis, Chief of the Saulteaux Indians and in grateful recognition of his good offices to the early Settlers and one of the first converts to Christianity of his race. He died in 1864 and his body rests in the old cemetery of St. Peter's where he was a devout worshipper. "Peguis has been a steady friend of the Settlement ever since its establishment and has never deserted its cause in its great reverses," said Lord Selkirk in 1817. Erected under the auspices of the Lord Selkirk Association of Rupert's Land 1924.

There is also a monument erected to his memory in Kildonan Park, and the plaque reads:

In Memory of Peguis Chief of the Saulteaux Indians
and in grateful recognition of his good office to the
early settlers. One of the first converts to Christianity of his race. He died in 1864 and his body
rests in the old cemetery where he was a devout
worshipper.

"Peguis has been a steady friend of the settlement
ever since its establishment and has never deserted
its cause in its greatest reverses." Lord Selkirk 1817.
Erected under the Auspices of the Lord Selkirk Association of Rupert's Land 1923.

This park occupies land where many of Peguis' Scottish friends farmed, and where he often danced at their
weddings and celebrated New Year's Day, accepting a
mug of rum from the man of the house, and from the
good wife, fresh buns rich with currants. Peguis and his
sons saw the settlers arrive and set up their wooden huts
on the land he considered his own, and he would not
allow his excitable young braves to harm the newcomers,
even when taunted by white men and those of mixed
blood for his tolerance.

His village of the little cornfields, so strategically situated at the south end of Lake Winnipeg where the Red
and the Netley meet, could have been a barrier to all
white settlement for many years if Peguis had not ex-
tended the hand of friendship.

The following year, 1865, my great great-grandfather's good friend, the Reverend William Cockran died at
Portage la Prairie. He was buried at St. Andrew's Church
not far from St. Peter's Parish.

Chapter 6

After Peguis died his son, Henry Prince, or Red Eagle as he was known to the Band, became Chief of the Saulteaux although he was by now middle-aged. Henry Prince had been educated at the mission school and attended the St. Peter's Church, and he raised his own sons in the Christian faith.

Two of the boys went to St. John's College in Winnipeg to study theology. Joseph died soon after his graduation but the Reverend William Henry Prince served as missionary-teacher for many years at St. Peter's. A third son, John, or 'Long Jake' as he was more familiarly called, remained at home to assist his father in his position as Chief.

The first test of Chief Henry Prince's loyalty to the settlers came in 1869 when Louis Riel rebelled against the North West's entry into Confederation and occupied the Hudson's Bay Company's headquarters at Upper Fort Garry. Chief Henry Prince met with Riel on more than one occasion and voiced his disapproval of the Métis' behavior. He was particularly annoyed when Riel called a general meeting, and refused to allow his speech, in French, to be translated into Cree.

When there were rumours of Riel taking over the Lower Fort Garry as well, Chief Henry Prince led one hundred men to the fort. Here the Canadian Government surveyors were billeted. Chief Henry Prince offered to assist the chief surveyor, Colonel S. Dennis, in suppressing the Métis uprising.

Colonel Dennis did not wish to engage Red River in civil war but he gratefully received a dozen Saulteaux as guards. Henry Prince kept his young men at St. Peter's and rejected all appeals from Louis Riel to join forces with him.

The Province of Manitoba was established in 1870 and the following summer the first treaty was signed between the natives and the Government of Canada.[1]

The name Mis-koo-ke-new, or Chief Henry Prince, appeared above those of ten other chiefs on this important document.

(A copy of this treaty is on page 69)

By 1875 the Canadian Government, having concluded Treaties Number One, Two, Three, Four and Five, realized that the payments to the Indians granted in the first two, were inadequate, and the figures were raised from three dollars to five dollars per annum. Furthermore the Government agreed to "make payments over and above such sum of $5.00, of $20 each and every year to each Chief, a suit of clothing every three years to each Chief, and each Headman of each band. . . ."[2]

Ever since the signing of the 1871 treaty that gave the lands known as the St. Peter's Reserve to the Saulteaux, there had been complaints from those of mixed

36

blood who claimed a prior right by virtue of possession of this same land. Their letters to Ottawa made the accusation that their property "had been handed out to the Indians."

After years of irate correspondence, Ottawa created a Board of Commissioners in 1885 to listen to the claims of both settlers and the Saulteaux. A rough rule of ownership was "no one who had not lived on the property and cultivated the land he claimed to own shall be entitled to a patent."

John, the Chief's son, travelled to Ottawa as his father's proxy to sign Canadian Government documents which were considered certain to appease all parties and conclude the St. Peter's Reserve dispute.

When Long Jake Prince was presented to Sir John A. MacDonald, the two men were startled by the fact they resembled one another enough to have been brothers. This so impressed the Prime Minister that as long as he lived he sent an annual gift to Long Jake at the Peguis Reserve where he was a Councillor.

By this date the Canadian Pacific Railway had reached East Selkirk where the transcontinental tracks were expected to cross the Red River. Much activity was created by the construction of the railway. There were saloons, blacksmith shops, flour mills and several hotels.

With the change in Federal Government the railway was rerouted through Winnipeg, and the white population in East Selkirk moved to the west side of the river where a road leading to Winnipeg had long since been established.

The Saulteaux remained at St. Peter's, content with the old quiet ways. The Reserve had prospered with many good homes, farmlands, schools and churches.

I was two years old when Chief Henry Prince died in 1902. His son, the Reverend William Henry Prince, my grandfather, became Chief. It was during this period that one of Chief Henry Prince's sons-in-law tried many times to break up the St. Peter's Reserve.

The Chief and his Council held meetings with the Band to discuss matters pertaining to the surrender of the Reserve. The majority of the Band were in favour of the surrender, while the Chief, and three of his four Councillors objected.

The election of a new Chief and Councillors took place about this time, and William Prince, a cousin of my grandfather was elected to fill the post. The former Chief, the Reverend William Henry Prince, became a Councillor. It was during this term of office that the agreement for the surrender of the Reserve was finally reached.

In 1909 terms had been agreed on for the surrender of roughly 48,000 acres, "being composed of the whole of St. Peter's Indian Reserve . . . ." for the sum of $5000.

The documents read in part:

A new Reserve for this Band shall be selected on Lake Winnipeg, to the extent of 75,000 acres of available land, but shall not include more than ten miles of water frontage. The Department is to make necessary survey of the lands to be patented, and the lands sold as soon as expedient after surrender, and

The author, photographed in 1945, at age 45 years.

First school at Peguis Reserve, built in early 1910's. Photograph taken in 1940's. L. to r. Florence Farmer, Missionary, Bertha Sutherland and baby, Loivey Stevenson, Violet Bear, Annabelle Bear (child), and Christie Sutherland.

One of the first homes built on new Peguis Reserve, belonging to Mr. and Mrs. Frank Stranger. *Courtesy Mrs. (Dorothy) Stranger.*

First treaty payment being made in 1872 at St. Peter's Reserve, north of Selkirk. *Courtesy Public Archives of Canada.*

the patents to issue upon application of the individual Indians, after the land is selected and properly designated.

The Department shall advance at the time of the surrender the sum of $5000 to be paid out of the first monies received from the sale of the lands.

A reasonable supply of agricultural implements and tools for use in the new Reserve shall be supplied, and distributed at the discretion of the Department.

The Department is to render reasonable assistance in removing to the new Reserve, in summer time, in any year within five years of the date of this surrender. . . .

And we, the said Chief and principal man of the said Band of Chippewa and Saulteaux and Cree Indians do on behalf of our people and ourselves, hereby ratify and confirm, whatever the Government may do, or cause to be lawfully done, in connection with the said lands and surrender.

Signed, sealed and delivered in the presence of —

Frank Pedley	Chief William Prince	seal
John Semmens	Councillor W. D. Harper	seal
O. I. Grain	Councillor W. H. Prince	seal
Ernest Raynor	Councillor John Prince	seal
	Councillor J. Williams	seal
	Councillor Wm. Asham Sr.	seal

So Chief William Prince and his Councillors, together with the Indian Agent and other Government officials, whose duty it was to protect the people on the Reserve from unfair practices, signed the surrender.

Many of the Indians protested. They declared that they had only been made aware of the proposal when four posters appeared on various buildings in town two days before the meeting was to be held. These read:

To the St. Peter's Band of Indians — Take notice, that a meeting of the male members of this Band of the full age of twenty-one (21) years, will be held at the Treaty grounds of this Reserve on Monday the 23rd day of September 1907 at 11 o'clock a.m. for the purpose of considering, deciding, and assenting to the release and surrender of St. Peter's Indian Reserve on the terms to be set forth at this meeting. (signed) Chief William Prince.

It was utterly impossible for all the residents of the Reserve to be made aware of this meeting. Many men were miles away hunting. Many others could not read the notice, which was written in English and not Cree.

The meeting was held in a schoolhouse too small to hold the 200 men who turned out. This made it necessary for those within the building to make known the progress of the meeting through the open window to those standing outside.

Eye-witness accounts were given by various respected men of the community whose knowledge of English was perfect. One of the most intelligent letters was written to Ottawa by William Asham, a former Chief of the Band. Briefly he says —

The meeting was held in an old school-house on

the Reserve, too small to hold more than half of those present. Those present representing the Government were Chief Justice Howell, Frank Pedley, Deputy Superintendent General of Indian Affairs, S. J. Jackson, M.P., E. Rayner of Selkirk, John Semmons, Inspector of Indian Agencies, J.O. Lewis, Indian Agent, and Dr. Grain.

When the meeting was called to order, Frank Pedley was selected to take the Chair, and I was called in from outside and requested by one of the gentlemen to act as Interpreter. This I declined to do stating I wanted a free hand, but William Henry Prince, one of the Councillors, acted as Interpreter and interpreted parts of the proceedings.

Mr. Pedley started to explain the condition of the surrender informing the meeting that he was sent by the Government to arrange for the surrender of the Reserve. Mr. Pedley explained to the meeting what the Government was willing to do if we would agree to surrender the Reserve. One proposition he made was that the Chief would receive 180 acres of land and each Councillor 120, and each Indian receive only 16 acres of land. I immediately demanded the reason why the Chief and Councillors should receive more land than the ordinary Indian. Mr. Pedley replied that they were getting the extra land for their recognition. I then stated the only recognition they had was the coat they wore and the extra money they receive annually. I also stated that they were not entitled to one acre more land than the ordinary Indian would receive but as the agreement of surrender was already prepared there was no change made at the time.

I further declared that at least two-thirds of the Indians present did not understand the conditions as stated by Mr. Pedley. I, understanding English, did most of the talking against the surrender of the Reserve and after talking several hours back and forward I demanded a vote to be taken. At this time there was no question that a large majority of the Band that were present were against the surrender, and expressed themselves loudly at times to this effect. Mr. Pedley and the Council and others interested refused to allow the vote to be taken that night and the meeting was adjourned until ten o'clock the next day at the same place.

William Asham's long letter continued to describe what took place the following day at the little schoolhouse:

I was surprised to find that some of those who had supported me strongly against the surrender the day before had been changed during the night. What caused this change God only knows, I don't. We adjourned for lunch after a good deal of talking, and Mr. W. D. Harper, Councillor asked me to have lunch with him at his home.

Mr. Harper was the son-in-law of the late Chief Henry Prince.

After lunch sitting in the school with the others

Harper slipped a piece of paper into my hand with the following words written in lead pencil by himself to the effect 'What would you think if you were to be made equal to a Councillor?' meaning of course that I would get as much land as a Councillor if I would agree to the surrender. I stated that I could not possibly agree. Before going into lunch, James Williams Councillor, came up to me and giving me a nudge whispered, 'Go and see Chief Justice Howell.' I replied 'No, I will not go near him.'

A moment later Asham was approached by the Member of Parliament S. J. Jackson, who drew the former Chief, William Asham, aside.

"Mr. Asham, you are strongly opposed to the surrender."

"Yes."

"What would you think if we were to make you equal with the Council? I will promise to get you a patent for the land within six weeks."

Asham rejected the offer:

I declared that if I had agreed I would have felt that I would be accepting a bribe to desert my friends who were protesting against the surrender. Now, soon after this, we were in the heat of a hot discussion in the matter regarding the surrender. Mr. Pedley during his speech at this time said "I have $5000 here," pointing to a satchel at his side. "If you agree to this surrender this money will be distributed among you, but if you don't agree to the surrender, I will take my satchel and go home and you won't get a cent." Then we were told the time had come to take a vote. Up to this time fully half of the Band present had not been able to get into the building and did not hear what had taken place. The building being too small to take the vote in, we were asked to go outside. Then Mr. John Semmons, the inspector of Indian agencies, spoke loudly in Cree saying — "All you that want $90 go to this side" — indicating where the Chief and Councillors were standing. "The others go to the opposite side."

The crowd separated not knowing what they were doing. After they were separated some of them moved from one side to the other. Mr. Semmons and myself started to count the votes that were against but when we got through counting we turned around to count the other side. I was told then that the other side had been counted. I did not know who counted the other side, and they claimed they had a majority of seven. I was astonished to hear this, and sized up the two sides and satisfied myself that there were a larger number standing on my side (opposers) than there was with the Chief and Councillors, but I had no opportunity whatever of counting the number that stood by the Chief and Councillors. I protested to Mr. Semmons, saying that he should not have said "You who want the $90 go on one side" but you should have said "you that *want to surrender* the Reserve go to one side, and you that don't want to surrender the Reserve go to the other side," then the people would have understood what they were voting for.

William Asham declared the vote irregular, and objected to the fact that when Mr. Pedley read the surrender it was in English and too fast, and that even he who knew English well found it difficult to understand the terms of the surrender:

> This was not interpreted to the Band in their own language, consequently few, if any, understood the conditions of the surrender. I am satisfied that Mr. Pedley and the others came determined to secure the surrender. It was all prepared without any consultation with the Band, they brought the $5000 with them. Without this money on the ground I am satisfied that never could they have secured the support they did in favour of the surrender.
>
> Immediately after the vote was taken the treaty was signed, and they commenced paying the money out... I have never ceased to protest against what I consider to be an outrage and the disinheriting of the Indians and sacrificing my birthright.
>
> And I make this solemn declaration conscientiously believing it to be true and knowing it to be of the same force and effect as if made under oath and by virtue of the Canada Evidence Act.

When the stunned opposers to the surrender realized what had taken place gloom and depression settled on the homeless people. The educated Indians who understood the full implications of the matter, placed their grievances before G. H. Bradbury, Member of Parliament for the area. Armed with sworn statements and proof of trickery and bribery by Government officials and land-sharks, Mr. Bradbury spent two days in the House in Ottawa laying bare this miserable act of broken faith before the Government.

Four men were chiefly implicated in this fraudulent acquisition of Reserve lands, acquired at $2 per acre, and which they frequently sold for $20. No Government action was ever taken to rescind this illegal purchase of Indian Reserve land. No effort was made to adjust the low prices paid to the Indians.

After the surrender was made the people had to move north one hundred miles to where the Fisher River empties into Lake Winnipeg. Unlike long-established St. Peter's Parish there were no houses here, no broken land, neither school nor church.

After the signing of the surrender of St. Peter's Reserve on September 24, 1907, the Dominion Lands Surveyors through the Chief Engineer, Mr. McLean, supervisor, made preparations to survey our new Reserve to be called Peguis, and the people began to move from St. Peter's in 1909.

My family was among the first group of forty to leave, travelling on the *S.S. City Of Selkirk* and the *S.S. Frederick*. It was now July and no time was lost in making a start on the new homes, and collecting hay for the livestock, in preparation for winter. The men worked tirelessly on the buildings during the wet weather. In spite of their efforts all were not completed before winter, and some families had to live with relatives until the following spring, when our own homes were finished.

I remembered that there were thirty-six houses completed in 1909, and the rest of our Band came to the new Reserve at a later date.

Living conditions were difficult. There was only one store, eight miles away at Fisher River, operated by a Mr. Roger. Transportation was very difficult and the storekeeper found it almost impossible to bring in enough supplies for the new settlers about Fisher River as well as for his old customers on the Fisher River Reserve established in 1871.

His only means of transportation was by sailboat and I recall that it was old and not very large. Our groceries were limited and had to be rationed. Flour was cut down to eight pounds per purchase per customer, and only a week's supply of fat could be bought at one time. Many of the newcomers were forced to deal elsewhere to get enough to eat.

The nearest town then was Gimli, seventy-five miles away by the old Indian trail, and a new road had to be cut from the new Peguis Reserve we were now on, as far as Vidir. When the men had completed this, supplies were brought in by ox team. We used oxen because the hay was of such poor quality that horses could not thrive on it. It usually took ten or eleven days to make the round trip from the Reserve to Gimli.

There was no employment for our men near the Reserve apart from wood-cutting. This was not new work to them, as they had already done a great deal of cutting around Tyndall, Whitemouth and West Selkirk.

Many of the people had to live in tents while cutting logs for their homes. Land had to be cleared before gardens and crops could be planted. The Government did not supply any agricultural implements or seed. The old people often talked of the past when the Reverend William Cockran had encouraged the Saulteaux to work the land by giving these needed items to the people at St. Peter's.

In order to start life on the Peguis Reserve our parents and grand-parents received Band funds from the Government, and spent several thousand dollars on establishing homes and schools.

After a number of years more land was cleared and cultivation started on the Reserve.

The Honourable G. H. Bradbury made the following comments on the St. Peter's Reserve surrender in the House of Commons on Wednesday April 13, 1910:

Mr. Speaker, before you leave the Chair, I desire to call the attention of the House to a matter of very serious importance, a matter that affects the honour of this country, regarding a transaction that ranks in my mind, high amongst the meanest ever committed by the Government. It was an outrage against everything that was fair, against everything that was decent between the Government of the day and its ward, the poor unfortunate Indians, who, this country believes, is watched over, guided and protected by the Government. The manner in which this Government has discharged its sacred trust towards the wards of the people is well exemplified by the way in which it manipulated and secured the surrender of the St. Peter's Reserve at Selkirk, which happens to be in my country.

The Honourable Member was armed with a good deal of ammunition and he used it to reveal what had taken place at St. Peter's in September 1907, presumably with the knowledge and consent of the Minister responsible for the Indian Department, the Honourable Frank Oliver. He read a letter written in Ottawa by Mr. Pedley, one month after the surrender had taken place. It was addressed to Mr. Oliver:

Pursuant to your instructions, I left Ottawa on the 17th ultimo, and reached Winnipeg on the 19th ult, to take up with the St. Peter's Band of Indians, near Selkirk the question of surrender of their Reserve at that place. When this Reserve, consisting of about 55,000 acres, was set aside in 1871, provision was made that the rights of the parties holding lands within the boundaries of the Reserve should be protected, and as a result of this some 5000 acres have been patented by parties other than Indians. In order to settle the remaining outstanding claims Chief Justice Howell of Manitoba appointed a commissioner in November 1906 for this purpose, and from several interviews with him I judge there would be from 1,500 to 2,000 acres still to be patented, thus leaving as belonging to the Reserve proper about 48,000 acres. This was the area that I dealt with in my negotiations with the Indians for a surrender.

Mr. Pedley's letter goes on to explain to the Minister of the Indian Department the sums of money granted the Chief and Councillors and the amount of land granted to each Indian. Mr. Bradbury continued his speech to the House — It will be seen that by this surrender the Government secured 48,000 acres of land. This land was all situated within a radius of 25 or 26 miles of the City of Winnipeg. . . . I have no hesitation in saying that 85% of this land is first class, and was the best land to be found in the province of Manitoba. This Government that boasts in this House, and out of it, that its policy is — the land for the settler and not for speculators — with this boast still warm on its lips, still ringing in the ears of the people of this country, lends itself to this scandalous transaction by which nearly 35,000 acres out of 48,000 acres passed into the hands of a few of its political friends for less than one-third of its actual value.

Mr. Bradbury declared that the settlers were "actually paying today eight and ten times as much for an acre of these lands as the Government allowed the speculators and party-heelers to secure for it from the Indian. This is the way in which this western policy of the Government works out. That the House may understand the conditions, I intend to lay before it facts which will show how this trick was worked."

In addition to his own observations Mr. Bradbury read a great many sworn testimonies and affidavits, all scathing condemnations of the treatment to Indians received at the hands of Government officials during and following

50

the surrender.

The Honourable Bradbury's speech to the House occupies 53 pages of Hansard on the subject of the St. Peter's Indian Reserve surrender. Today, contrary to the obligations of the treaty stipulations, the St. Peter's surrender has never been settled and still waits for the Royal Commission.

We know that from time immemorial the Indians assisted the white man. When they first set foot on this continent the Indians guided them in their explorations, such men as David Thompson, Jacques Cartier and Simon Fraser. Without the Indian the white man would have starved or drowned. There were dangerous rapids and falls to portage, and death was certain if one tried to shoot these rapids along the rivers. The Indians also fought side by side with their white brothers even before the treaties were established.

Then came the day the Government, through Queen Victoria's representatives, negotiated terms of a treaty with the Indians. Those treaties contained many solemn promises, such as implements, schools, etc. Promises sound good. They were told: "Her Majesty shall have you as her own children and you will be protected at all times for you will be wards of Her Majesty's Government, for you have done a wonderful thing to surrender your country to Her Government and this shall stand for all time." (see Treaty No. 1, p. 69)

The answer given them was that no Government, and not even the Queen herself, could alter or bring in a new law on top of the treaty foundation. The treaties were firmly made and our people, my ancestors, were assured that the Queen's word was the truth, and would never be broken. No other words could explain better how many Indians feel about the Treaties than Carole Nahmabin's poem:

Broken Promises

My people, a very proud and noble race,
Thanked the Great Spirit with upturned face.
They were happy with their land, their sons, and daughters,
Watching the sunlight dance on peaceful, clear waters.
Listening to the wind whisper through tall, green pines
A good people, of sound body and mind.
They walked free with nature, their mother,
And wanting no evil to come to one another.

Then came invaders . . . . the white man.
Destroying, killing, making false promises, was their plan.
No longer did the sunlight dance on peaceful waters,
But the rivers ran red with the blood that came from slaughters.
The wind didn't whisper through the pines anymore;
Not the way it did before.

It now carried the scent of the white eyes,
Who, with their forked tongues told many lies.

They said they were our brothers.
Is it not written that we treat them as they do
    others?
Maybe we just don't understand their way.
But why is it we always have to pay?
Who was it that brought the fire water?
Now they say, "Look at the Indian, see the totter".
I guess we'll never truly understand
Why they want all our land.

Then they put us on a reservation,
Saying it was for our own preservation.
This will always be your land.
It will belong to you, and all your band,
Freedom to hunt and fish forever.
With their word, said, "This will fail no, never."
Also you won't ever pay any tax.
But their promises, they are all of wax.

Our medical rights will soon be gone.
Is there anything else that they can pawn?
They say they want desegregation
For purposes of education.
We need a licence to hunt even in season.
Another broken promise, with a real reason.
Now, my red brothers, are you wise?
Or will you listen to more of their lies?

My people have very little left,
All because of the white man's theft.
The treaties that they signed long in the past
Are like their words — they never did last.

As the long cold winters turn to spring
Their empty words will always ring.
By now we know the white man and his need.
We will remember him always by his greed.

Carole Nahmabin
Kettle Point Reserve

Chapter 7

The Canadian Pacific Railway had completed their railway line to Arborg in 1909, and by 1910 some merchants moved in and built their stores and commenced doing business, and thus ended the journey to Gimli. This carried on until 1914 when the Canadian Northern Railway completed its line to Hodgson.

Mr. John Ross started his store in 1912 at Marble Ridge and carried on until other merchants started their business in 1914. The first merchants in Hodgson in 1914 were S. Sigurdson and George Lahoud.

That winter, men started to cut and deliver number one tamarack for 65 cents per cord and continued till spring breakup in 1915.

Let me go back to 1909 when we first arrived here. We had neither schools, churches, nor a post-office. Schools were built of logs and completed before the school term in September 1911. One was built at North Peguis and the other at South Peguis. The teacher at North Peguis was one of the members of our Reserve in the person of Angus Prince, a great great-grandson of Chief Peguis.

The teacher of South Peguis was an Englishman by

the name of Henry Francis. The third school was built at Central Peguis around 1922.

In 1910 the adults of North Peguis held meetings seeking ways and means to get a post office. After several meetings they decided to petition the Postmaster General in Ottawa requesting the post office, and this they did. It was not long until they got a reply stating they should select a name. Many suggestions for the name were given. Finally, my grandfather, the Reverend William Henry Prince, told those attending the meeting they should call it this:

Mr. James Asham (known to us as Dill Asham) was the one chosen for the first postmaster. We should change the "i" in Dill to "a" making it dall, and add the first two letters of Asham to make the word Dallas. This is how we got the name Dallas. Others chose Eagle Nest. When these two names were sent to Ottawa Dallas was approved. There was already a post office named Eagle Nest on the Winnipeg River in Manitoba.

Church services were held in private homes up to 1911. When the schools were completed, services were held in them up to 1922. By that time two churches were completed, one in South Peguis and the other at Central Peguis. The South church was named St. Matthews, and the one at Central was named St. Peter's. The church at North Peguis was built around 1925 and called All Saints. Those are Anglican churches. The Roman Catholic church was built in 1919. The first Apostolic Chapel, now known as Pentecostal, was built in 1912 in North

Peguis. The one in the South was built in 1943.

Our first Anglican clergyman was the Reverend Edward Thomas, one-time member of the Peguis Reserve. He stayed on here from 1909 to 1911 when the Reverend Canon Maurice Sanderson replaced him, and we have had many clergymen since.

A large gathering was held in 1944 at the Centenary celebration of Bishop Mountain's visit to Red River. I was present, as well as my uncle A. E. Prince, and his cousin Joseph A. Harper.

In 1916 the Reverend William Henry Prince had lost his wife Catherine Bauer (my grandmother). This was a great grief to the old clergyman, and he continued to mourn her loss until his own death on September 4, 1929. He was survived by one daughter Mrs. Catherine Thompson, my mother, and one son Albert E. Prince, seventeen grandchildren and eleven great-grandchildren.

The Centennial of Chief Peguis' death, held in 1964, was the biggest gathering of its kind in the history of the Indian Church along the banks of the Red River at the St. Peter's Reserve. Hundreds of people from all over the country came to honour his memory.

The Saulteaux received only $5000.00 and 73,000 acres of new land at the time of the St. Peter's surrender in 1908, yet Band funds had to be used to pay for the relocation of the people. Materials for homes and farm machinery had to be purchased out of that money to get the people started. Today the system is very different.

Any man wishing to farm must buy his own implements. In this way keen interest is taken and more efforts are being made to increase farming on the Peguis Reserve, which is the largest in Manitoba. The Indians now own a number of tractors, threshing outfits and combines, and trucks. Almost half the population own family cars.

The economy of the reserve was greatly improved when The Monarch Wear of Canada, Ltd. opened a factory. It employs men and women from both the Fisher River and Peguis Reserves. It took only three or four days to teach the women how to use the sewing machines and to train the cloth-cutters, then the Company was in full operation.

At the opening of the factory, at which I spoke, I said that we felt very fortunate to have such an opportunity for employment.

Chief Peguis would be very proud of many of his descendants. They fought bravely in both World Wars and before that in the Boer War. In fact, the Indians of Canada have done their duty in all wars that have taken place from time immemorial. They have won medals for bravery and many citations to honour them for their services. My cousin Sergeant Thomas Prince, who won so many medals is not the only man who won many medals. Many an Indian hero has done so. Canada should be proud of her native sons.

The most outstanding fighter in recent wars is Thomas George Prince, holder of six campaign ribbons and ten medals. Born in Petersfield on October 25, 1915, Tommy, as he is known to his friends, grew up in the country so well known to Chief Peguis about the Interlake and Red River.

He enlisted with the Royal Canadian Engineers in 1940, then became a member of the First Canadian Parachute Battalion in Europe. Tommy was twice decorated by King George VI at Buckingham Palace in 1944. He was later transferred to the special force of Canadian-American Paratroopers.

He was awarded the Military Medal for his gallantry at the Anzio beachhead. The United States presented him with the Silver Star for valour during the invasion of Southern France, when he set up 1500 yards of telephone wire in enemy territory, manned an artillery post alone for twenty-four hours and destroyed four enemy posts.

Tommy Prince was discharged in 1945, and in '46 and '47 represented the Manitoba Indians at Ottawa on the Indian Problem Discussions. His army service took him overseas five times from the North Pacific to the Mediterranean, Africa, Europe and Korea. He was slightly wounded in Korea in 1952.

In 1953 while walking by the Red River early one Sunday summer morning he heard cries for help and saved a man from drowning.

He now makes his home in Winnipeg.

One of the most outstanding women descendants of Chief Peguis is Mrs. William Clements, or Amy, as she is affectionately known to hundreds of Manitobans.

Born near St. Peter's old stone church sixty-six years ago, Amy was one of the first Indian women on the staff of the Indian and Métis Friendship Centre, established in Winnipeg in 1959. For nine years Amy commuted between her home and the Centre, a distance of twenty-five miles. In 1969, when Selkirk opened a native Friendship Centre, Amy Clements was the logical choice as executive-director. She served there until her retirement.

She is a woman of delightful disposition and remarkable physical stamina, as proven by her participation in a twenty-seven mile walkathon a year before her retirement.

In Manitoba's Centennial celebrations of 1970, Amy Clements was presented to Queen Elizabeth and members of the Royal Family at St. Peter's church beside the grave of her great great-grandfather Chief Peguis.

She wore the traditional ceremonial costume, a white gown fringed and beaded in tiny canoe and maple leaf motifs. She had on brightly beaded moccasins and headband, and carried a fan of eagle feathers.

The same year, Amy's services to her people were recognized when she was elected Woman of the Year by the Women's Sales and Advertising Club of Winnipeg.

Chapter 8

This is some personal data.

I was born at St. Peter's Reserve September 4, 1900. My father was George Thompson of Fairford, Manitoba, and my mother was Catherine Margret Prince of St. Peter's, Manitoba.

I attended school at St. Peter's from September 1905 up to the end of the school term June 1909. From September 1909 I attended school at Fisher River Reserve for two years. Beginning with the school term in September 1911, I attended the Peguis North School until the end of June 1915. From there I left for the Elkhorn Industrial School and attended from September 1915 until the end of June 1916.

I joined the Armed Forces of the Canadian Expeditionary Force and was with this outfit till the end of hostilities and was demobilized January 11, 1919.

After demobilization, I hired out to work for the Northern Fish Company on May 25, 1919 and was stationed at Big Black River, I then met my brother William, who himself had just returned from the Armed Forces in Siberia. It was a happy reunion.

After the fishing season was over, we came home to

Peguis and started to put up hay, for our own livestock and for sale. We did well on our venture. Afterwards I was engaged in different lines of employment, such as working with a surveyor party, in fishing camps, and logging both in pulp and wood fuel camps. I worked for the Winnipeg Cartage Company at Pine Falls and for the Abitibi Pulp and Paper Company until March 1945.

On May 31, 1934, I married Nancy Gaudet at Fort Alexander. The following year we became the proud parents of our son Albert. To our regret three other children died at an early age.

I am proud to say we have two lively teenage grandsons, and both are attending school.

At present we have a lovely school situated one mile north of the Fisher River Agency. It consists of 25 classrooms and 28 teachers who teach the children from pre-kindergarten to Grade IX. There is also a fine gymnasium, a workshop and a kitchen. The kitchen is used also to train the women in cooking, sewing and handicrafts. My wife is one of the instructors.

We launched a program to build an indoor skating arena. We had meetings on this matter and made good progress. It opened in late 1970, and was our Centennial Project.

For years the Department of Indian Health Services promised to build an integrated hospital on our Reserve adjacent to the town of Hodgson. I was instructed to organize a hospital board in 1970 and as a result we will have a very fine Hospital Complex in 1973.

The Peguis Band Council Administration Building was officially opened July 8, 1971, and a library was opened the following year. There are many new homes, and there is a telephone office adjacent to public buildings. The best news of all perhaps is that the Peguis Central School will have a Grade X class in the fall of 1973.

I now reside in Peguis, and I am living in the fourth house since I returned. I will continue to live in my present home until I am gone from this world of ours.

I began to organize the Indians of Manitoba in 1934 when I was living at Fort Alexander. I had a hard time organizing the Indians, but I had the ball rolling by the time I resigned in October 1967. I am happy to say that the young men who took over are doing an excellent job. Before I resigned I was offered financial assistance to carry on the Indian administration. Due to ill health I had no alternative but to refuse. I am still active and ready to assist the Indian Brotherhood whenever my help is required.

I was elected to the Peguis Band Council March 20, 1953 and served as a Councillor until March 20, 1961 when I ran for the chieftainship. I was elected by a large majority and I am still Chief of the Reserve. I will carry on as long as my health permits me to do so.

I made seven trips to Ottawa as a representative of the Manitoba Brotherhood during the time I was president. During one visit, in 1964, I was asked to present our case of the St. Peter's Surrender, in which we ceded all our lands in 1907 for the paltry sum of $5,000.00.

Five years after I had organized the Manitoba Indian Brotherhood their Majesties King George VI and Queen Elizabeth visited Winnipeg on May 24th, 1939. I invited many Chiefs and Headmen from tribes in Manitoba, Western Ontario, the northern United States and Saskatchewan to take part in a parade along the streets of Winnipeg to celebrate this historic occasion.

Two hundred and twenty men came with their wonderful doeskin costumes and feathered headdresses. We marched from Redwood Ave. down Main Street and along Portage Avenue to Polo Park, which at that time was a horse-race track with lots of seats and bleachers.

The Royal procession moved from Assiniboine Park down Portage Avenue to Polo Park where eight thousand school children stood waving flags. The King and Queen left their limousine and walked in front of the grandstand, and a school-band from Minnesota played the National Anthem.

Then the Royal couple walked down in front of us. I am sure that we made quite a picture in our Ojibway, Cree, Saulteaux, and Sioux costumes. Some of the men even wore paint on their faces. One of the Chiefs, Kesik, wore a Distinguished Service Medal of the First World War. Another, Chief Hotain, a Sioux warrior, had fought under Sitting Bull against the American Long Knives in 1876. He offered a pipe of peace to King George. Chief Hotain was eighty-five years old, and His Majesty thanked him graciously for the gift.

This was a great day for all of us, and no doubt the King and Queen were pleased by the showing that two hundred and twenty of us made in full ceremonial dress.

On September 15, 1965 I was appointed member of the Regional Advisory Council of Manitoba, and before the end of 1965 I was again appointed to the National Advisory Board. This gave me power to represent the Indians on both the federal and provincial political levels.

During "Expo 67" I made two trips to Montreal. Both trips were enjoyable, as I saw wonderful displays which the various nations had in their respective pavilions.

Along with 200 distinguished guests, I was invited to a luncheon at Kildonan Park Pavilion on June 6, 1967, in honour of Her Royal Highness Princess Alexandra and her husband, The Hon. Angus James Ogilvy. It was a great honour for me, and an occasion I shall never forget.

On July 3, 1967, at a Peguis Day celebration, Lord Selkirk and Lady Selkirk were present. I presented the Earl with a peace-pipe and a headdress on behalf of the Women's Auxiliary of St. Peter's Parish. He, in turn, made me a member of the Douglas clan. After the ceremony at this historical old St. Peter's Church, I had lunch along with approximately 200 guests, with the tenth Earl Lord Selkirk, marking the 150th year since my great great-grandfather, Chief Peguis, negotiated the terms of the treaty with the fifth Earl, Thomas Douglas, Lord Selkirk in 1817.

The most outstanding visitors came on July 14, 1970 — Her Royal Highness Queen Elizabeth II, and members of her family. We celebrated Peguis Day on that date instead of on June 19th, the day in 1816 when the Seven Oaks massacre occurred. I presented Her Majesty with the history of Chief Peguis. It was a great honour to me and to my people to make this presentation to Her Majesty and a wonderful occasion to remember in days to come.

After meeting with the Second World War veterans of St. Peter's Parish, the Queen and her royal family boarded the *M.S. Lord Selkirk II*, and cruised along the Red River.

On December 18, 1969 I was promoted Senator by the Indian Brotherhood, and the Regional Director of Indian Affairs, Manitoba region, by R. M. Connelly, in the office of the Manitoba Indian Brotherhood.

Make a survey. You will find out what we have in Canada. There are Indian lawyers, teachers, clergymen, stenographers and Indians in other professions too numerous to mention. Anyone is welcome to tour my Reserve and find out the kind of Indians we have living on Peguis.

As you have heard on radio and read in the public press people of all races in Manitoba have different ideas as to the founders or builders of the province of Manitoba. I have the building and opening of our great province summarized thus —

It began when Chief Peguis arrived from Sault Ste. Marie with his small band of Indians to start building their homes and till the soil for gardens until the Selkirk colonists arrived from Scotland in 1812. Peguis and the colonists became great friends and co-operated in every

66

way possible to make this new land the best agricultural centre in Western Canada. The colonists had a hard time building up the province, though no attempt was made to enter into Confederation in 1867, when Eastern Canada was first introduced into Confederation,

Louis Riel came into the picture. He gave the early settlers advice in regard to entering this part of the west into Confederation. An attempt was made by Riel to form the province, give it a name and introduce the proposed entry to the Fathers of Confederation asking to have Manitoba amalgamated into Confederation.

This is how Manitoba became a province in 1870.

To sum up, it would have been Peguis, Lord Selkirk colonists, and Louis Riel, who made it possible for Manitoba to become a province.

In the early days the descendants of Peguis had patience and made their survival possible by hunting and trapping for the Hudson's Bay Company. In the autumn of each year they went on a buffalo hunting trip and when a herd was spotted they killed enough buffalo to cure the meat for future use, and the hides for wearing apparel, etc.

My grandfather used to tell me about the Red River cart brigades. There were so many of them on the hunting trips that you could hear the cart wheels screech for a mile or two. There were always riders sent a few miles ahead of the brigade. When they spotted a herd of buffalo they retreated and met the hunters that were behind. They halted for the night and the next day made the kill, and remained there till all the meat was cured.

This was done by cutting the meat into strips and hanging them on stages or racks built high enough to keep the meat from the dogs.

When the meat was cured by the sun and the wind, it was pounded into powder and mixed with wild berries and bear-fat if available. The mixture was called pemmican and the women packed it in bags or pouches made from buffalo-hide. Pemmican would keep for years and was the staple food of both Indian and white man when the hunting was poor, or food had to be carried for a great distance.

Life is different with us today, and the people have prospered. On Peguis Reserve the men have modern equipment for fishing and farming, and cars and trucks. There are comfortable homes, good schools, and a hospital and Senior Citizen Home for those who need these services.

The memory of Chief Peguis is still honoured by the Saulteaux in the land he chose and lived in peaceably most of his life. He was a great leader, and his descendants have followed the example he set to prove themselves good citizens.

Treaty No. 1

ARTICLES OF A TREATY made and concluded this third day of August in the year of Our Lord one thousand eight hundred and seventy-one, between Her Most Gracious Majesty the Queen of Great Britain and Ireland by Her Commissioner, Wemyss M. Simpson, Esquire, of the one part, and the Chippewa and Swampy Cree Tribes of Indians, inhabitants of the country within the limits hereinafter defined and described, by their Chiefs chosen and named as hereinafter mentioned, of the other part.

Whereas all the Indians inhabiting the said country have pursuant to an appointment made by the said Commissioner, been convened at a meeting at the Stone Fort, otherwise called Lower Fort Garry, to deliberate upon certain matters of interest to Her Most Gracious Majesty, of the one part, and to the said Indians of the other, and whereas the said Indians have been notified and informed by Her Majesty's said Commissioner that it is the desire of Her Majesty to open up to settlement and immigration a tract of country bounded and described as hereinafter mentioned, and to obtain the consent thereto of her Indian subjects inhabiting the said tract, and to make a treaty and arrangements with them so that there may be peace and good will between them and Her Majesty, and that they may know and be assured of what allowance they are to count upon and receive year by year from Her Majesty's bounty and benevolence.

And whereas the Indians of the said tract, duly convened in council as aforesaid, and being requested by Her Majesty's said Commissioner to name certain Chiefs and Headmen who should be authorized on their behalf to conduct such negotiations and sign any treaty to be founded thereon, and to become responsible to Her Majesty for the faithful performance by their respective bands of such obligations as should be assumed by them, the said Indians have thereupon named the following persons for that purpose, that is to say:—

Mis-koo-kenew or Red Eagle (Henry Prince), Ka-ke-ka-penais, or Bird for ever, Na-sha-ke-penais, or Flying down bird, Na-na-wa-nanaw, or Centre of Bird's Tail, Ke-we-tayash, or Flying round, Wa-ko-wush, or Whip-poor-will, Oo-za-we-kwun, or Yellow Quill,—and thereupon in open council the different bands have presented their respective Chiefs to His Excellency the Lieutenant Governor of the Province of Manitoba and of the North-West Territory being present at such council, and to the said Commissioner, as the Chiefs and Headman for the purposes aforesaid of the respective bands of Indians inhabiting the said district hereinafter described; and whereas the said Lieutenant Governor and the said Commissioner then and there received and acknowledged the persons so presented as Chiefs and Headmen for the purpose aforesaid; and whereas the said Commissioner has proceeded to negotiate a treaty with the said Indians, and the same has finally been agreed upon and concluded as follows, that is to say: —

The Chippewa and Swampy Cree Tribes of Indians and all other the Indians inhabiting the district hereinafter described and defined do hereby cede, release, surrender and yield up to Her Majesty the Queen and successors forever all the lands included within the following limits, that is to say: —

Beginning at the international boundary line near its junction with the Lake of the Woods, at a point due north from the centre of Roseau Lake; thence to run due north to the centre of Roseau Lake; thence northward to the centre of White Mouth Lake, otherwise called White Mud Lake; thence by the middle of the lake and the middle of the river issuing therefrom to the mouth thereof in Winnipeg River; thence by the Winnipeg River to its mouth; thence westwardly, including all the islands near the south end of the lake, across the lake to the mouth of Drunken River; thence westwardly to a point on Lake Manitoba half way between Oak Point and the mouth of Swan Creek; thence across Lake Manitoba in a line due west to its western shore; thence in a straight line to the crossing of the rapids on the Assiniboine; thence due south to the international boundary line; and thence eastwardly by the said line to the place of beginning. To have and to hold the same to Her said Majesty the Queen and Her successors for ever; and Her Majesty the Queen hereby agrees and undertakes to lay aside and reserve for the sole and exclusive use of the Indians the following tracts of land, that is to say: For the use of the Indians belonging to the band of which Henry Prince, otherwise called Mis-koo-ke-new is the Chief, so much of land on both sides of the Red River, beginning at the south line of St. Peter's Parish, as will furnish one hundred and sixty acres for each family of five, or in that proportion for larger or

70

smaller families; and for the use of the Indians of whom Na-sha-ke-penais, Na-na-wa-nanaw, Ke-we-tayash and Wa-ko-wush are the Chiefs, so much land on the Roseau River as will furnish one hundred and sixty acres for each family of five, or in that proportion for larger or smaller families, beginning from the mouth of the river; and for the use of the Indians of which Ka-ke-ka-penais is the Chief, so much land on the Winnipeg River above Fort Alexander as will furnish one hundred and sixty acres for each family of five, or in that proportion for larger or smaller families, beginning at a distance of a mile or thereabout above the Fort; and for the use of the Indians of whom Oo-za-we-kwun is Chief, so much land on the south and east side of the Assiniboine, about twenty miles above the Portage, as will furnish one hundred and sixty acres for each family of five, or in that proportion for larger or smaller families, reserving also a further tract enclosing said reserve to comprise an equivalent to twenty-five square miles of equal breadth, to be laid out round the reserve, it being understood, however, that if, at the date of the execution of this treaty, there are any settlers within the bounds of any lands reserved by any band, Her Majesty reserves the right to deal with such settlers as She shall deem just, so as not to diminish the extent of land allotted to the Indians.

And with a view to show the satisfaction of Her Majesty with the behaviour and good conduct of Her Indians parties to this treaty, She hereby, through Her Commissioner, makes them a present of three dollars for each Indian man, woman and child belonging to the bands here represented.

And further, Her Majesty agrees to maintain a school on each reserve hereby made whenever the Indians of the reserve should desire it.

Within the boundary of Indian reserves, until otherwise enacted by the proper legislative authority, no intoxicating liquor shall be allowed to be introduced or sold, and all laws now in force or hereafter to be enacted to preserve Her Majesty's Indian subjects inhabiting the reserves or living elsewhere from the evil influence of the use of intoxicating liquors shall be strictly enforced.

Her Majesty's Commissioner shall, as soon as possible after the execution of this treaty, cause to be taken an accurate census of all the Indians inhabiting the district above described, distributing them in families, and shall in every year ensuing the date hereof, at some period during the month of July in each year, to be duly notified to the Indians and at or near their respective reserves, pay to each Indian family of five persons the sum of fifteen dollars Canadian currency, or in like proportion for a larger or smaller family, such payment to be made in such articles as the Indians shall require of blankets, clothing, prints (assorted colours), twine or traps, at the current cost price in Montreal, or otherwise, if Her Majesty shall deem the same desirable in the interests of Her Indian people, in cash.

And the undersigned Chiefs do hereby bind and pledge themselves and their people strictly to observe this treaty and to maintain perpetual peace between themselves and Her Majesty's white subjects, and not to interfere with the property or in any way molest the persons of Her Majesty's white or other subjects.

IN WITNESS WHEREOF, Her Majesty's said Commissioner and the said Indian Chiefs have hereunto subscribed and set their hand and seal at Lower Fort Garry, this day and year herein first above named.

Signed, sealed and delivered in the
presence of, the same having
been first read and explained:

ADAMS G. ARCHIBALD,
   Lieut.-Gov. of Man. and
   N.W. Territories.
JAMES McKAY, *P.L.C.*
A. G. IRVINE, *Major.*
ABRAHAM COWLEY,
DONALD GUNN, *M.L.C.*
THOMAS HOWARD, *P.S.*
HENRY COCHRANE,
JAMES McARRISTER,
HUGH McARRISTER,
E. ALICE ARCHIBALD,
HENRI BOUTHILLIER,

WEMYSS M. SIMPSON,   [L.S.]
   Indian Commissioner,
MIS-KOO-KEE-NEW, or RED EAGLE
      his
   (HENRY PRINCE), x
      mark
KA-KE-KA-PENAIS (or BIRD FOR EVER),
      his
   WILLIAM PENNEFATHER, x
      mark

   NA-SHA-KE-PENNAIS, or
      his
   FLYING DOWN BIRD, x
      mark

NA-HA-WA-NANAN, or
             his
CENTRE OF BIRD'S TAIL, x
             mark

             his
KE-WE-TAY-ASH, or FLYINGROUND, x
             mark

             his
WA-KO-WUSH, or WHIP-POOR-WILL, x
             mark

             his
OO-ZA-WE-KWUN, or YELLOW QUILL, x
             mark

Memorandum of things outside of the Treaty which were prom-ised at the Treaty at the Lower Fort, signed the third day of August, A.D. 1871

For each Chief who signed the treaty, a dress distinguishing him as Chief.

For braves and for councillors of each Chief a dress; it being supposed that the braves and councillors will be two for each Chief.

For each Chief, except Yellow Quill, a buggy.

For the braves and councillors of each Chief, except Yellow Quill, a buggy.

In lieu of a yoke of oxen for each reserve, a bull for each, and a cow for each Chief; a boar for each reserve and a sow for each Chief, and a male and female of each kind of animal raised by farmers, these when the Indians are prepared to re-ceive them.

A plough and a harrow for each settler cultivating the ground.

These animals and their issue to be Government property, but to be allowed for the use of the Indians, under the super-intendence and control of the Indian Commissioner.

The buggies to be the property of the Indians to whom they are given.

The above contains an inventory of the terms concluded with the Indians.

WEMYSS M. SIMPSON,
MOLYNEUX St. JOHN,
A. G. ARCHIBALD,
JAS. McKAY.

———

COPY *of a Report of a Committee of the Honourable the Privy Council, approved by His Excellency the Governor General in Council on the 30th April, 1875.*

On a memorandum dated 27th April, 1875, from the Honourable the Minister of the Interior, bringing under consideration the very unsatisfactory state of affairs arising out of the so-called "outside promises" in connection with the Indian Treaties Nos. 1 and 2, Manitoba and North-west Territories, concluded, the former on the 3rd August, 1871, and the latter on 21st of the same month, and recommending for the reasons stated:—

1st. That the written memorandum attached to Treaty No. 1 be considered as part of that Treaty and of Treaty No. 2, and that the Indian Commissioner be instructed to carry out the promises therein contained, in so far as they have not yet been carried out, and that the Commissioner be advised to inform the Indians that he has been authorized so to do.

2nd. That the Indian Commissioner be instructed to inform the Indians, parties to Treaties Nos. 1 and 2, that, while the Government cannot admit their claim to any thing which is not set forth in the treaty, and in the memorandum attached thereto, which treaty is binding alike upon the Government and upon the Indians, yet, as there seems to have been some misunderstanding between the Indian Commissioner and the Indians in the matter of Treaties Nos. 1 and 2, the Government, out of good feeling to the Indians and as a matter of benevolence, is willing to raise the annual payment to each Indian under Treaties Nos. 1 and 2, from $3 to $5 per annum, and make payment over and above such sum of $5, of $20 each and every year to each Chief, and a suit of clothing every three years to each Chief and each Headman, allowing two Headmen to each band, on the express understanding, however, that each Chief or other Indian who shall receive such increased annuity or annual payment shall be held to abandon all claim whatever against the Government in connection with the so-called "outside promises," other than those contained in the memorandum attached to the treaty.

The Committee submit the foregoing recommendation for Your Excellency's approval:

W. A. HIMSWORTH,
Clerk Privy Council.

Certified,
    W. A. HIMSWORTH,
      Clerk Privy Council.

We, the undersigned Chiefs and Headmen of Indian bands, representing bands of Indians who were parties to the Treaties Nos. 1 and 2, mentioned in the report of the Committee of the Queen's Privy Council of Canada, above printed, having had communication thereof, and fully understanding the same assent thereto and accept the increase of annuities therein mentioned, on the condition therein stated, and with the assent and approval of their several bands, it being agreed, however, with the Queen's Commissioners, that the number of braves and councillors for each Chief shall be four, as at present, instead of two, as printed 1875.

TREATY No. 2, 23rd August, 1875.
In the presence of the following:

ALEX MORRIS, *L.G.* [L.S.]	Representing East-Manitoba or Elm
JAMES McKAY,	Point:
JAMES F. GRAHAM,	his
ISAAC COWIE,	SON-SONSE, x *Chief*,
FRANCIS FIELD,	mark
JOHN A. DAVIDSON,	
CHARLES WOOD,	

NA-KA-NA-WA-TANG, x his mark

PA-PA-WE-GUN-WA-TAK, x his mark
Councillors.

Representing Fairford Prairie:
MA-SAH-KEE-YASH, x *Chief,* his mark

DAVID MARSDEN, x *Councillor.* his mark

JOSEPH SUMNER, x *Councillor.* his mark

Fairford Mission:

RICHARD WOODHOUSE, *Chief,*

JONN ANDERSON, *Councillor.*

JOHN THOMPSON, x *Councillor.* his mark

Formerly Crane River and now Ebb and Flow Lake:

PENAISE, x *Chief,* his mark
(son of deceased Broken Finger.)

BAPTISTE, x *Councillor,* his mark

KAH-NEE-QUA-NASH, x *Councillor,* his mark

Representing Water Hen Band:

KA-TAH-KAK-WA-NA-YASS, x Chief,
his
mark

WA-WAH-KOW-WEK-AH-POW, x Councillor.
his
mark

Representing the Turtle River and Valley
River and Riding Mountain:

KEE-SICK-KOO-WE-NIN, x Chief,
his
mark
(in place of Mekis, dead.)

KEE-SAY-KEE-SICK, x Councillor,
his
mark

NOS-QUASH, x Brave,
his
mark

BAPTISTE, x Brave.
his
mark

Representing the St. Peter's Band:

MIS-KOO-KE-NEW (or Red Eagle), x
his
mark

MA-TWA-KA-KEE-TOOT, x
his
mark

I-AND-WAY-WAY, x
his
mark

MA-KO-ME-WE-KUN, x
his
mark

AS-SHO-AH-MEY, x
his
mark

No. 124³.

We, the undersigned Chiefs and Headmen of Indian bands representing bands of Indians who were parties to the Treaties Nos. 1 and 2, mentioned in the report of a Committee of the Queen's Privy Council of Canada, "as printed on the other side of this parchment," having had communication thereof and fully understanding the same, assent thereto and accept the increase of annuities therein mentioned on the condition therein stated, and with the assent and approval of their several bands, it being agreed, however, with the Queen's Commissioners, that the number of braves and councillors for each Chief shall be four, as at present, instead of two, as printed 1875.

Signed near Fort Alexander, on the Indian Reserve, the twenty-third day of August in the year of Our Lord one thousand eight hundred and seventy-five.

his
KAKEKEPENAIS, x or
mark
(WILLIAM PENNEFATHER),

Witnesses:

J. A. N. PROVENCHER,
  Indian Commissioner.
J. DUBUC,
A. DUBUC,
JOSEPH MONKMAN, *Interpreter.*
WM. LOUNT,
H. L. REYNOLDS.

his
JOSEPH x KENT,
mark

his
PETANAQUAGE, x or
mark
(HENRY VANE),

his
PETER x HENDERSON,
mark

his
KAY-PAYAHSINISK, x
mark

Signed at Broken Head River, the twenty-eighth day of August, in the year of our Lord one thousand eight hundred and seventy-five.

Witnesses:

J. A. N. PROVENCHER,
  Indian Commissioner.
J. DUBUC,
H. L. REYNOLDS,
DANIEL DEVLIN,
HENRY COOK.

his
NASHAKEPENAIS, x
mark

his
AHKEESEEKWASKEMG, x
mark

<pre>
                              his
NAYWAHEHEEKEEGIK, x
                             mark
                              his
MAYJAHKEEGEEQUAN, x
                             mark
                  his
PAYSAUGA, x
            mark
</pre>

CHAPTER NOTES

Chapter 1
1. My great great-grandfather was not called Peguis by the Selkirk Settlers. He was known to them as Peeg-wace, and the story of how he acquired his name is quite interesting. He said that he was abandoned when an infant and found on a pile of wood-chips by an elderly woman who raised him as her own son. She named him Peeh-quaa-is, or Little Chip.[2]
Various spellings appear in early Manitoba records: Pigwys, Pigeois, and Be-gou-ais. In time, the name Peeh-quaa-is became simply Peguis.
2. When the first Selkirk Settlers arrived at Red River in 1812 and 1814 Pockwa-now was in his mid-twenties. He was a good-natured youth and liked to chat with the farmers and their families. He often told them of the summer of the small-pox plague, and how he kept himself alive shooting birds and rabbits with his little bow and arrows. He considered himself very fortunate to have been found by the Saulteaux and adopted into their band.
3. John Tanner, the white boy who was kidnapped from his home in Ohio and adopted by an Ottawa woman who was the daughter of a Chieftain, has left a very interesting story of his life.
John Tanner wrote on page 29 of his story — "In one day she sold 120 beaver skin with a large quantity of buffalo robes, dressed and smoked skins and other articles for rum."
4. P. 154 of John Tanner story.

Chapter 2
1. Journal of Archibald McDonald. This was the man who led the first families from Scotland to Red River.
2. The Lord Selkirk Papers
3. Father Dugas Life of Marie Anne Lajimoniere. (His spelling)
4. John Tanner's story

Chapter 3
1. *The Nor'Wester*
2. This document may be seen at the Manitoba Archives.
3. Ibid
4. *The Nor'Wester*

Chapter 4
1. Reverend John West's Journal
2. Ibid
3. Nicholas Garry's Diary
4. Rev. Wm. Cockran's Red River Journal
5. Ibid

Chapter 5

1. May be seen at Manitoba Archives.
2. Ibid. This Bible bears the notation — "Presented to the Chippewa Chieftain by Archdeacon Cockran probably in 1838, on the occasion of his first professing Christianity and receiving by G. H. Gunn from a great grandson of Peguis, Charles Thomas Parisien. Lot 98 St. Peter's Manitoba. May 30/1928."
2. Ibid
3. This chair is now on display at the Lower Fort Garry Museum. St. Andrews Manitoba.
4. The Rev. John Smithurst Journal. Red River.
5. *The Nor'Wester*

Chapter 6

1. See Treaty Number One.
2. Found in Adhesions for Treaty Number One and Two.

From chapter Six to the end sources are chiefly from family and private papers, letters, memories, etc.

BIBLIOGRAPHY

Cockran, William: *Red River Papers.*

Dugas, Fr. Georges: *La Première Canadienne au Nord-Ouest* (English trans. *Life of Marie-Anne Lajimoniere*).

Evans, James: *Papers.*

Garry, Nicholas: *Diary.*

Hansard, Ottawa, April 3, 1910, pages 7009-7064.

Henry, Alexander, the Younger: *Journal.*

James, Edwin: *Narrative of the Captivity and Adventures of John Tanner during Thirty Years' Residence Among the Indians.*

Kane, Paul: *Wanderings of an Artist.*

Macdonell, Miles: *Journal.*

McDonald, Archibald: *Journal.*

Lord Selkirk Papers, Provincial Archives of Manitoba.

The Nor'wester.

The Selkirk Enterprise.

Smithurst, John: *Red River Journal.*

West, John: *Substance of a Journal during a Residence at the Red River Colony.*

Winnipeg Free Press.

INDEX